EXTRACTS FOR THE TIMES

MARY—THE SECOND EVE

FROM THE WRITINGS OF

JOHN HENRY NEWMAN

COMPILED

BY

SISTER EILEEN BREEN, F.M.A.

TAN Books and Publishers, Inc.
Rockford, Illinois

Photograph and extracts with the permission of the Fathers of the Birmingham Oratory.

Originally published in 1977 by Sister Eileen Breen, F.M.A. and reprinted in 1982 by TAN Books and Publishers, Inc. from her edition.

ISBN: 0-89555-181-0

Printed and bound in the United States of America.

TAN Books and Publishers, Inc.
P.O. Box 424
Rockford, Illinois 61105

1982

CONTENTS

PREFACE

This pamphlet consists of a series of extracts from some of the books written by John Henry Newman. The extracts are arranged systematically so as to provide continuous reading of his key-thoughts and key-explanations about the Blessed Virgin. There is no word other than Newman's in the pamphlet—except where he himself quotes the early Fathers of the Church.

A very important part of the pamphlet is that of the quotations Newman gives—chiefly in the section on THE SECOND EVE, but also in that on THEOTOCOS—from the early Fathers of the Church, who had received the teaching of the Apostles. It was his reading of the Fathers which made him realise that *their* teaching—being the teaching of the early Church—was the true teaching,—teaching based on the truth of Scripture.

On 29th January, 1868, Newman, when commenting on the acceptance—in England—of his Apologia, wrote: " . . . Perhaps He wishes me to do nothing new, but He is creating an opportunity for what I have already written to work. . . . Perhaps my name is to be turned to account as a sanction and outset by which others, who agree with me in opinion, should write and publish instead of me, and thus begin the transmission of views in religious and intellectual matters congenial with my own to the generation after me." (From THE LIFE OF JOHN HENRY CARDINAL NEWMAN, by Wilfrid Ward, London, 1912. Vol. II p. 204).

H.H. Pope Paul VI used part of the above quotation in his address to the Newman Symposium (7th April, 1975), and he added: " . . . the present time can be considered in a special way as Newman's hour, in which with confidence in Divine Providence, he placed his great hopes and expectations. . . . it is precisely the present moment that suggests, in a particularly pressing and persuasive way, the study and diffusion of Newman's thought. . . . May his prayer become ours too: 'Enable me to believe as if I saw; let me have Thee always before me as if Thou wert always bodily and sensibly present. Let me ever hold communion with Thee, my hidden, but my living God.' " (Meditations and Devotions).

18th June, 1977.   SISTER EILEEN BREEN, F.M.A.,
Feast of The Immaculate Heart of Mary.   Compiler.

SOURCES

I A LETTER TO THE REV. E. B. PUSEY, D.D.,
ON HIS RECENT EIRENICON
BY JOHN HENRY NEWMAN, D.D., OF THE ORATORY

(Longmans, Green, Reader, and Dyer, 1866).

II MEDITATIONS AND DEVOTIONS OF THE LATE
CARDINAL NEWMAN

(Longman, Green and Co., 1893).

III DISCOURSES ADDRESSED TO MIXED CONGREGATIONS
BY JOHN HENRY NEWMAN

(Dublin: James Duffy, Wellington Quay and
London: 22 Paternoster Row, 1862).

IV SAYINGS OF CARDINAL NEWMAN

Originally published 1890.

(Carraig Books (Reprints 3—1976),
Blackrock, Co. Dublin).

V TO HENRY WILBERFORCE   Maryvale, January 19th, 1948.

(The Letters and Diaries of John Henry Newman—
Volume XII)

(Thomas Nelson and Sons Ltd.).

INTRODUCTORY EXTRACTS

. . . there just now seems a call on me . . . to avow plainly what I do and what I do not hold about the Blessed Virgin, that others may know, did they come to stand where I stand, what they would, and what they would not, be bound to hold concerning her. (I p. 27).

.　　.　　.

Though I hold, as you know, a process of development in Apostolic truth as time goes on, such development does not supersede the Fathers, but explains and completes them. And, in particular, as regards our teaching concerning the Blessed Virgin, with the Fathers I am content; . . . the Fathers are enough for me. (I p. 26).

.　　.　　.

I fully grant that *devotion* towards the Blessed Virgin has increased among Catholics with the progress of centuries; I do not allow that the *doctrine* concerning her has undergone a growth, for I believe that it has been in substance one and the same from the beginning. (I p. 28).

.　　.　　.

The faith is everywhere one and the same; but a large liberty is accorded to private judgment and inclination as regards matters of devotion. (I p. 30).

.　　.　　.

I recollect one saying among others of my confessor, a Jesuit father, one of the holiest, most prudent men I ever knew. He said that we could not love the Blessed Virgin too much, if we loved our Lord a great deal more. (I p. 23).

.　　.　　.

1

THE SECOND EVE

What is the great rudimental teaching of Antiquity from its earliest date concerning her? By "rudimental teaching" I mean the *primâ facie* view of her person and office, the broad outline laid down of her, the aspect under which she comes to us, in the writings of the Fathers. She is the **Second Eve**. Now let us consider what this implies. Eve had a definite, essential position in the First Covenant. The fate of the human race lay with Adam; he it was who represented us. It was in Adam that we fell; though Eve had fallen, still, if Adam had stood, we should not have lost those supernatural privileges which were bestowed upon him as our first father. Yet though Eve was not the head of the race, still, even as regards the race, she had a place of her own; for Adam, to whom was divinely committed the naming of all things, entitled her **"the Mother of all the living"**, a name surely expressive, not of a fact only, but of a dignity; but further, as she thus had her own general relation to the human race, so again had she her own special place as regards its trial and its fall in Adam. In those primeval events, Eve had an integral share. **"The woman, being seduced, was in the transgression."** She listened to the Evil Angel; she offered the fruit to her husband, and he ate of it. She co-operated, not as an irresponsible instrument, but intimately and personally in the sin; she brought it about. As the history stands, she was a *sine-qua-non,* a positive, active, cause of it. And she had her share in its punishment; in the sentence pronounced on her, she was recognised as a real agent in the temptation and its issue, and she suffered accordingly. In that awful transaction there were three parties concerned,—the serpent, the woman, and the man; and at the time of their sentence, an event was announced for the future, in which the three same parties were to meet again, the serpent, the woman, and the man; but it was to be a second Adam and a second Eve, and the new Eve was to be the mother of the new Adam. **"I will put enmity between thee and the woman, and between thy seed and her seed."** The Seed of the woman is the Word Incarnate, and the Woman, whose seed or son He is, is His mother Mary. This interpretation, and the parallelism it involves, seem to me undeniable; but at all events (and this is my point) the parallelism is the doctrine of the Fathers, from the earliest times; and, this being established, we are able, by the position and office of Eve in our fall, to determine the position and office of Mary in our restoration.

2

I shall adduce passages from their writings, with their respective countries and dates; and the dates shall extend from their births or conversions to their deaths, since what they propound is at once the doctrine which they had received from the generation before them, and the doctrine which was accepted and recognised as true by the generation to whom they transmitted it.

First, then, St. Justin Martyr (A.D. 120-165), St. Irenæus (120-200), and Tertullian (160-240). Of these Tertullian represents Africa and Rome; St. Justin represents Palestine; and St. Irenæus Asia Minor and Gaul;—or rather he represents St. John the Evangelist, for he had been taught by the Martyr St. Polycarp, who was the intimate associate as of St. John, so of the other Apostles.

1. St. Justin: —

"We know that He, before all creatures, proceeded from the Father by His power and will, . . . and by means of the Virgin became man, that by what way the disobedience arising from the serpent had its beginning, by that way also it might have an undoing. For Eve, being a virgin and undefiled, conceiving the word that was from the serpent, brought forth disobedience and death; but the Virgin Mary, taking faith and joy, when the Angel told her the good tidings, that the Spirit of the Lord should come upon her and the power of the Highest overshadow her, and therefore the Holy One that was born of her was Son of God, answered, 'Be it to me according to Thy word.' "
—*Tryph.* 100.

2. Tertullian: —

"God recovered His image and likeness, which the devil had seized, by a rival operation. For into Eve, as yet a virgin, had crept the word which was the framer of death. Equally into a virgin was to be introduced the Word of God which was the builder-up of life; that, what by that sex had gone into perdition, by the same sex might be brought back to salvation. Eve had believed the serpent; Mary believed Gabriel; the fault which the one committed by believing, the other by believing has blotted out."
—*De Carn. Christ.* 17.

3

3.   St. Irenæus: —

"With a fitness, Mary the Virgin is found obedient, saying,
'Behold Thy handmaid, O Lord; be it to me according to Thy word.'
But Eve was disobedient; for she obeyed not, while she was yet a
virgin. As she, having indeed Adam for a husband, but as yet being
a virgin . . . becoming disobedient, became the cause of death both
to herself and to the whole human race, so also Mary, having the
predestined man, and being yet a Virgin, being obedient, became
both to herself and to the whole human race the cause of salvation.
. . . And on account of this the Lord said, that the first should be
last and the last first. And the Prophet signifies the same, saying,
'Instead of fathers you have children.' For, whereas the Lord, when
born, was the first-begotten of the dead, and received into His bosom
the primitive fathers, He regenerated them into the life of God, He
Himself becoming the beginning of the living, since Adam became
the beginning of the dying. Therefore also Luke, commencing the
line of generations from the Lord, referred it back to Adam, signifying that He regenerated the old fathers, not they Him, into the
Gospel of life. And so the knot of Eve's disobedience received its
unloosing through the obedience of Mary; for what Eve, a virgin,
bound by incredulity, that Mary, a virgin, unloosed by faith."
—*Adv. Haer.* iii. 22. 34.

And again: —

"As Eve by the speech of an Angel was seduced, so as to flee
God, transgressing His word, so also Mary received the good tidings
by means of the Angel's speech, so as to bear God within her, being
obedient to His word. And, though the one had disobeyed God, yet the
other was drawn to obey God; that of the virgin Eve the Virgin Mary
might become the advocate. And, as by a virgin the human race had
been bound to death, by a virgin it is saved, the balance being
preserved, a virgin's disobedience by a virgin's obedience."
—*Ibid.* v. 19.

Now what is especially noticeable in these three writers, is, that
they do not speak of the Blessed Virgin merely as the physical
instrument of our Lord's taking flesh, but as an intelligent, responsible

4

cause of it; her faith and obedience being accessories to the Incarnation, and gaining it as her reward. As Eve failed in these virtues, and thereby brought on the fall of the race in Adam, so Mary by means of them had a part in its restoration. . . . not to go beyond the doctrine of the Three Fathers, they unanimously declare that she was *not* a mere instrument in the Incarnation, such as David, or Judah, may be considered; they declare she co-operated in our salvation not merely by the descent of the Holy Ghost upon her body, but by specific holy acts, the effect of the Holy Ghost within her soul; that, as Eve forfeited privileges by sin, so Mary earned privileges by the fruits of grace; that, as Eve was disobedient and unbelieving, so Mary was obedient and believing; that, as Eve was a cause of ruin to all, Mary was a cause of salvation to all; that as Eve made room for Adam's fall, so Mary made room for our Lord's reparation of it; and thus, whereas the free gift was not as the offence, but much greater, it follows that, as Eve co-operated in effecting a great evil, Mary co-operated in effecting a much greater good.

And, besides the run of the argument, which reminds the reader of St. Paul's antithetical sentences in tracing the analogy between Adam's work and our Lord's work, it is well to observe the particular words under which the Blessed Virgin's office is described. Tertullian says that Mary **"blotted out"** Eve's fault, and **"brought back the female sex"**, or **"the human race, to salvation"**; and St. Irenæus says that **"by obedience she was the cause or occasion"** (whatever was the original Greek word) **"of salvation to herself and the whole human race"**; that by her the human race is saved; that by her Eve's complication is disentangled; and that she is Eve's Advocate, or friend in need. It is supposed by critics, Protestant as well as Catholic, that the Greek word for Advocate in the original was Paraclete; it should be borne in mind, then, when we are accused of giving Our Lady the titles and offices of her Son, that St. Irenæus bestows on her the special Name and Office proper to the Holy Ghost.

So much as to the nature of this triple testimony; now as to the worth of it. For a moment put aside St. Irenæus, and put together St. Justin in the East with Tertullian in the West. I think I may assume that the doctrine of these two Fathers about the Blessed Virgin, was the received doctrine of their own respective times and places; for writers after all are but witnesses of facts and beliefs, and as such they are treated by all parties in controversial discussion. Moreover, the coincidence of doctrine which they exhibit, and again, the antithetical completeness of it, show that they themselves did not originate it. The next question is, Who did? for from one definite organ or source, place or person, it must have come. Then we must inquire, what length of time would it take for such a doctrine to have extended, and to be received, in the second century over so wide an area; that is, to be received before the year 200 in Palestine, Africa, and Rome. Can we refer the common source of these local traditions to a date later than that of the Apostles, St. John dying within thirty or forty years of St. Justin's conversion and Tertullian's birth? Make what allowance you will for whatever possible exceptions can be taken to this representation; and then, after doing so, add to the concordant testimony of these two Fathers the evidence of St. Irenæus, which is so close upon the School of St. John himself in Asia Minor. "A three-fold cord", as the wise man says, "is not quickly broken." Only suppose there were so early and so broad a testimony, to the effect that our Lord was a mere man, the son of Joseph; should we be able to insist upon the faith of the Holy Trinity as necessary to salvation? Or supposing three such witnesses could be brought to the fact that a consistory of elders governed the local churches, or that each local congregation was an independent Church, or that the Christian community was without priests, could Anglicans maintain their doctrine that the rule of Episcopal succession is necessary to constitute a Church? And then recollect that the Anglican Church especially appeals to the ante-Nicene centuries, and taunts us with having superseded their testimony.

4.   St. Cyril of Jerusalem (315-386) speaks for Palestine: —

"Since through Eve, a virgin, came death, it behoved, that through a Virgin, or rather from a Virgin, should life appear; that, as the Serpent had deceived the one, so to the other Gabriel might bring good tidings."
—*Cat.* xii. 15.

5.   St. Ephrem Syrus (he died 378) is a witness for the Syrians proper and the neighbouring Orientals, in contrast to the Græco-

Syrians. A native of Nisibis on the further side of the Euphrates, he knew no language but Syriac.

"**Through Eve, the beautiful and desirable glory of men was extinguished; but it has revived through Mary.**"
—*Opp. Syr.* ii. p. 318.

Again: —

"**In the beginning, by the sin of our first parents, death passed upon all men; today, through Mary we are translated from death unto life. In the beginning, the serpent filled the ears of Eve, and the poison spread thence over the whole body; today, Mary from her ears received the champion of eternal happiness: what, therefore, was an instrument of death, was an instrument of life also.**"
—iii. p. 607.

6. St. Epiphanius (320-400) speaks for Egypt, Palestine, and Cyprus: —

"**She it is, who is signified by Eve, enigmatically receiving the appellation of the Mother of the living. . . . It was a wonder that after the fall she had this great epithet. And, according to what is material, from that Eve all the race of man on earth is generated. But thus in truth from Mary the Life itself was born in the world, that Mary might bear living things, and become the Mother of living things. Therefore, enigmatically, Mary is called the Mother of living things. . . . Also, there is another thing to consider as to these women, and wonderful,—as to Eve and Mary. Eve became a cause of death to men . . . and Mary a cause of life; . . . that life might be instead of death, life excluding death which came from the woman, viz. He who through the woman has become our life.**"
—*Haer.* 78. 18.

7. By the time of St. Jerome (331-420), the contrast between Eve and Mary had almost passed into a proverb. He says (*Ep.* xxii. 21, *ad Eustoch.*), "**Death by Eve, life by Mary.**" Nor let it be supposed that he, any more than the preceding Fathers, considered the Blessed

Virgin a mere physical instrument of giving birth to our Lord, who is the Life. So far from it, in the Epistle from which I have quoted, he is only adding another virtue to that crown which gained for Mary her divine Maternity. They have spoken of faith, joy, and obedience; St. Jerome adds, what they had only suggested, virginity. After the manner of the Fathers in his own day, he is setting forth the Blessed Mary to the high-born Roman Lady, whom he is addressing, as the model of the virginal life; and his argument in its behalf is, that it is higher than the marriage-state, not in itself, viewed in any mere natural respect, but as being the free act of self-consecration to God, and from the personal religious purpose which it involves.

"Higher wage", he says, "is due to that which is not a compulsion, but an offering; for, were virginity commanded, marriage would seem to be put out of the question; and it would be most cruel to force men against nature, and to extort from them an angel's life." —20.

I do not know whose testimony is more important than St. Jerome's, the friend of Pope Damasus at Rome, the pupil of St. Gregory Nazianzen at Constantinople, and of Didymus in Alexandria, a native of Dalmatia, yet an inhabitant, at different times of his life, of Gaul, Syria, and Palestine.

8. St. Jerome speaks for the whole world, except Africa; and for Africa in the fourth century, if we must limit so world-wide an authority to place, witnesses St. Augustine (354-430). He repeats the words as if a proverb, **"By a woman death, by a woman life"** *(Opp. t. v. Serm. 232)*; elsewhere he enlarges on the idea conveyed in it. In one place he quotes St. Irenæus's words as cited above *(adv. Julian i. n. 5)*. In another he speaks as follows: —

"It is a great sacrament that, whereas through woman death became our portion, so life was born to us by woman; that, in the case of both sexes, male and female, the baffled devil should be tormented, when on the overthrow of both sexes he was rejoicing; whose punishment had been small, if both sexes had been liberated in us, without our being liberated through both."
—*Opp. t.* vi. *De Agon. Christ.* c.24.

9. St. Peter Chrysologus (400-450), Bishop of Ravenna, and one of the chief authorities in the 4th General Council: —

"Blessed art thou among women; for among women, on whose womb Eve, who was cursed, brought punishment, Mary, being blest, rejoices, is honoured, and is looked up to. And woman now is truly made through grace the Mother of the living, who had been by nature the mother of the dying. . . . Heaven feels awe of God, Angels tremble at Him, the creature sustains Him not, nature sufficeth not; and yet one maiden so takes, receives, entertains Him, as a guest within her breast, that, for the very hire of her home, and as the price of her womb, she asks, she obtains peace for the earth, glory for the heavens, salvation for the lost, life for the dead, a heavenly parentage for the earthly, the union of God Himslf with human flesh."
—*Serm.* 140.

It is difficult to express more explicitly, though in oratorical language, that the Blessed Virgin had a real meritorious co-operation, a share which had a **"hire"** and a **"price"**, in the reversal of the fall.

10. St. Fulgentius, Bishop of Ruspe in Africa (468-533). The Homily which contains the following passage, is placed by Ceillier (t. xvi. p. 127) among his genuine works: —

"In the wife of the first man, the wickedness of the devil depraved her seduced mind; in the mother of the Second Man, the grace of God preserved both her mind inviolate and her flesh. On her mind it conferred the most firm faith; from her flesh it took away lust altogether. Since then man was in a miserable way condemned for sin, therefore without sin was in a marvllous way born the God-man."
—*Serm.* 2, p. 124. *De Dupl. Nativ.* . . .

Such is the rudimental view, as I have called it, which the Fathers have given us of Mary, as the **Second Eve**, the Mother of the living: I have cited ten authors. I could cite more, were it necessary: except the two last, they write gravely and without any rhetoric. I allow that the two last write in a different style, since the extracts I have made are from their sermons; but I do not see that the colouring conceals the outline. And after all, men use oratory on great subjects, not on small;—nor would they, and other Fathers whom I might quote, have lavished their high language upon the Blessed Virgin, such as they gave to no one else, unless they knew well that no one else had such claims, as she had, on their love and veneration.   (I p. 33-46).

.   .   .

THE IMMACULATE CONCEPTION

By the Immaculate Conception of the Blessed Virgin is meant the great revealed truth that she was conceived in the womb of her mother, St. Anne, without original sin.[1] . . . to her grace came,[2] . . . from the first moment of her being, as it had been given to Eve.[2]

([1]II p. 10, [2]I p. 50).

.   .   .

It is so difficult for me to enter into the feelings of a person who *understands* the doctrine of the Immaculate Conception, and yet objects to it, that I am diffident about attempting to speak on the subject. . . .

Does not the objector consider that *Eve* was created, or born, *without* original sin? Why does not *this* shock him? Would he have been inclined to *worship* Eve in that first estate of hers? Why, then, Mary?

Does he not believe that St. John Baptist had the grace of God— i.e. was regenerated, even before his birth? What do we believe of Mary, but that grace was given her at a still earlier period? *All* we say is, that grace was given her from the first moment of her existence.

We do not say that she did not owe her salvation to the death of her Son. Just the contrary, we say that she, of all mere children of Adam, is in the truest sense the fruit and the purchase of His Passion. He has done for her more than for anyone else. To others He gives grace and regeneration at a *point* in their earthly existence; to her from the very beginning.

10

We do not make her *nature* different from others. . . . A more abundant gift of grace made her what she was from the first. . . . She and we are both simply saved by the grace of Christ. (II p. 115-118).

. . .

. . . I ask, was not Mary as fully endowed as Eve? is it any violent inference, that she, who was to co-operate in the redemption of the world, at least was not less endowed with power from on high, than she who, given as a helpmate to her husband, did in the event but co-operate with him for its ruin? If Eve was raised above human nature by that indwelling moral gift which we call grace, is it rash to say that Mary had a greater grace? And this consideration gives significance to the Angel's salutation of her as **"full of grace"**,—an interpretation of the original word which is undoubtedly the right one, as soon as we resist the common Protestant assumption that grace is a mere external approbation or acceptance, answering to the word "favour", whereas it is, as the Fathers teach, a real inward condition or superadded quality of soul. And if Eve had this super-natural inward gift given her from the first moment of her personal existence, is it possible to deny that Mary too had this gift from the very first moment of her personal existence? I do not know how to resist this inference: —well, this is simply and literally the doctrine of the Immaculate Conception. I say the doctrine of the Immaculate Conception is in its substance this, and nothing more or less than this (putting aside the question of degrees of grace); and it really does seem to me bound up in that doctrine of the Fathers, that Mary is the **Second Eve**. (I p. 48-49).

. . .

It is to me a most strange phenomenon that so many learned and devout men stumble at this doctrine, and I can only account for it by supposing that in matter of fact they do not know what we mean by the Immaculate Conception; . . . It is a great consolation to have reason for thinking so,—for believing that in some sort the persons in question are in the position of those great Saints in former times, who are said to have hesitated about it, when they would not have hesitated at all, if the word "Conception" had been clearly explained in that sense in which now it is universally received. I do not see how anyone who holds with Bull the Catholic doctrine of the supernatural endowments of our first parents, has fair reason for doubting our doctrine about the Blessed Virgin. It has no reference whatever to her parents, but simply to her own person; it does but affirm that, together with the nature which she inherited from her parents, that is, her own nature, she had a superadded fulness of grace, and that from the first moment of her existence. Suppose Eve had stood the trial, and not lost her first grace; and suppose she had eventually had children, those children from the first moment of their existence would, through divine bounty, have received the same privilege that she had ever had; that is, as she was taken from Adam's side, in a garment, so to say, of grace, so they in turn would have received what may be called an immaculate conception. They would have been conceived in grace, as in fact they are conceived in sin. What is there difficult in this doctrine? What is there unnatural? Mary may be called a daughter of Eve unfallen. You believe with us that St. John Baptist had grace given to him three months before his birth, at the time that the Blessed Virgin visited his mother. He accordingly was *not* immaculately conceived, because he was alive before grace came to him; but our Lady's case only differs from his in this respect, that to her grace came, not three months merely before her birth, but from the first moment of her being, as it had been given to Eve.

But it may be said, How does this enable us to say that she was conceived without *original sin?* If Anglicans knew what we mean by original sin, they would not ask the question. Our doctrine of original sin is not the same as the Protestant doctrine. "Original sin", with us, cannot be called sin, in the ordinary sense of the word "sin"; it is a term denoting the imputation of Adam's sin, or the state to which Adam's sin reduces his children; but by Protestants it is understood to be sin, in the same sense as actual sin. We, with the Fathers, think of it as something negative, Protestants as something positive. Protestants hold that it is a disease, a change of nature, a poison internally corrupting the soul, and propagated from father to son, after the manner of a bad constitution; and they fancy that we ascribe a different nature from ours to the Blessed Virgin, different from that of her parents, and from that of fallen Adam. We hold nothing of the kind; we consider that in Adam she died, as others; that she was included, together with the whole race, in Adam's sentence; that she incurred his debt, as we do; but that, for the sake of Him who was to redeem her and us upon the Cross, to her the debt was remitted by anticipation, on her the sentence was not carried out, except indeed as regards her natural death, for she died when her time came, as others. All this we teach, but we deny that she had original sin; for by original sin we mean, as I have already said, something negative, viz., this only, the *deprivation* of that supernatural unmerited grace which Adam and Eve had on their creation—deprivation and the consequences of deprivation. Mary could not merit, any more than they, the restoration of that grace; but it was restored to her by God's free bounty, from the very first moment of her existence, and thereby, in fact, she never came under the original curse, which consisted in the loss of it. And she had this special privilege, in order to fit her to become the Mother of her and our Redeemer, to fit her mentally, spiritually for it; so that, by the aid of the first grace, she might so grow in grace, that when the Angel came, and her Lord was at hand, she might be **"full of grace"**, prepared, as far as a creature could be prepared, to receive Him into her bosom.

I have drawn the doctrine of the Immaculate Conception, as an immediate inference, from the primitive doctrine that Mary is the **Second Eve**. . . . If controversy had in earlier days so cleared the subject as to make it plain to all, that the doctrine meant nothing else than that, in fact, in her case the general sentence on mankind was not carried out, and that, by means of the indwelling in her of divine grace from the first moment of her being (and this is all the decree of 1854 has declared), I cannot believe that the doctrine would have ever been opposed; for an instinctive sentiment has led Christians jealously to put the Blessed Mary aside when sin comes into discussion. This is expressed in the well-known words of St. Augustine, All have sinned **"except the Holy Virgin Mary, concerning whom, for the honour of the Lord, I wish no question to be raised at all, when we are treating of sins."** *(de Nat. et Grat.* 42); (I p. 49-53).

.   .   .

Now, as to the doctrine of the Immaculate Conception, it was *implied* in early times, and never *denied.* In the Middle Ages it *was* denied by St. Thomas and by St. Bernard, but they took the phrase in a different sense from that in which the Church now takes it. They understood it with reference to Our Lady's mother, . . . whereas *we* do not speak of the Immaculate Conception except as relating to Mary; and the other doctrine (which St. Thomas and St. Bernard did oppose) *is* really heretical. (II p. 120).

.   .   .

Many, many doctrines are far harder than the Immaculate Conception. The doctrine of Original Sin is indefinitely harder. Mary just has *not* this difficulty. It is *no* difficulty to believe that a soul is united to the flesh *without* original sin; the great mystery is that any, that millions on millions, are born with it. Our teaching about Mary has just one difficulty less than our teaching about the state of mankind generally. (II p. 125).

.   .   .

We, as the children of Adam, are heirs to the consequences of his sin, and have forfeited in him that spiritual robe of grace and holiness which he had given him by his Creator at the time that he was made. In this state of forfeiture and disinheritance we are all of us conceived and born; and the ordinary way by which we are taken out of it is the Sacrament of Baptism.

But Mary *never* was in this state; she was by the eternal decree of God exempted from it. From eternity, God, the Father, Son, and Holy Ghost, decreed to create the race of man, and, foreseeing the fall of Adam, decreed to redeem the whole race by the Son's taking flesh and suffering on the Cross. In that same incomprehensible, eternal instant, in which the Son of God was born of the Father, was also the decree passed of man's redemption through Him. He who was born from Eternity was born by an eternal decree to save us in Time, and to redeem the whole race; and Mary's redemption was determined in that special manner which we call the Immaculate Conception. It was decreed, not that she should be *cleansed* from sin, but that she should, from the first moment of her being, be *preserved* from

14

sin; so that the Evil One never had any part in her. Therefore she was a child of Adam and Eve as if they had never fallen; . . . (II p. 11-12).

. . .

EXALTATION

Here let us suppose that our first parents had overcome in their trial; and had gained for their descendants for ever the full possession, as if by right, of the privileges which were promised to their obedience, —grace here and glory hereafter. Is it possible that those descendants, pious and happy from age to age in their temporal homes, would have forgotten their benefactors? Would they not have followed them in thought into the heavens, and gratefully commemorated them on earth? The history of the temptation, the craft of the serpent, their steadfastness in obedience,—the loyal vigilance, the sensitive purity of Eve,—the great issue, salvation wrought out for all generations,—would have been never from their minds, ever welcome to their ears. This would have taken place from the necessity of our nature.

. . . the Saints are ever in our sight, and not as mere ineffectual ghosts, but as if present bodily in their past selves. It is said of them, **"Their works do follow them"**; what they were here, such are they in heaven and in the Church. As we call them by their earthly names, so we contemplate them in their earthly characters and histories. Their acts, callings, and relations below, are types and anticipations of their mission above. Even in the case of our Lord himself, whose native home is the eternal heavens, it is said of Him in His state of glory, that He is **"a Priest for ever"**; and when He comes again, He will be recognised by those who pierced Him, as being the very same that He was on earth. The only question is, whether the Blessed Virgin had a part, a real part, in the economy of grace, whether, when she was on earth, she secured by her deeds any claim on our memories; for, if she did, it is impossible we should put her away from us, merely because she is gone hence, and not look at her still, according to the measure of her earthly history, with gratitude and expectation. If, as St. Irenæus says, she did the part of an Advocate, a friend in need, even in her mortal life, if, as St. Jerome and St. Ambrose say, she was on earth the great pattern of Virgins, if she had a meritorious share in bringing about our redemption, if her maternity was earned by her faith and obedience, if her Divine Son was subject to her, and if she stood by the Cross with a mother's heart and drank in to the full those sufferings which it was her portion to gaze upon, it is impossible that we should not associate these characteristics of her life on earth with her present state of blessedness; and this surely she anticipated, when she said in her hymn that all generations should call her blessed. (I p. 53-56).

.   .   .

. . . it is to the point to inquire, whether the popular astonishment, excited by our belief in the Blessed Virgin's present dignity, does not arise from the circumstance that the bulk of men, engaged in matters of the world, have never calmly considered her historical position in the gospels, so as rightly to realise what that position imports. . . . I shall take what perhaps you may think a very bold step,—I shall find the doctrine of our Lady's present exaltation in Scripture.

I mean to find it in the vision of the Woman and Child in the twelfth chapter of the Apocalypse. . . . (I p. 56-57).

.   .   .

The Virgin and Child is *not* a mere modern idea; on the contrary, it is represented again and again, as every visitor to Rome is aware, in the paintings of the Catacombs. Mary is there drawn with the Divine Infant in her lap, she with hands extended in prayer, He with His hand in the attitude of blessing. No representation can more forcibly convey the doctrine of the high dignity of the Mother, and, I will add, of her power over her Son. Why should the memory of His time of subjection be so dear to Christians, and so carefully preserved? The only question to be determined, is the precise date of these remarkable monuments of the first age of Christianity. That they belong to the centuries of what Anglicans call the "undivided

Church" is certain; but lately investigations have been pursued, which place some of them at an earlier date than anyone anticipated as possible. . . . the earliest . . . to the very age of the Apostles. . . . it is lawful for me, though I have not the positive words of the Fathers on my side, to shelter my own interpretation of the Apostle's vision under the fact of the extant pictures of Mother and Child in the Roman Catacombs. . . . when we speak of a doctrine being contained in Scripture, we do not necessarily mean that it is contained there in direct categorical terms, but that there is no other satisfactory way of accounting for the language and expressions of the sacred writers, concerning the subject-matter in question, than to suppose that they held upon it the opinion which we hold,—that they would not have spoken as they have spoken, *unless* they held it. For myself I have ever felt the truth of this principle, as regards the Scripture proof of the Holy Trinity; I should not have found out that doctrine in the sacred text without previous traditional teaching; but when once it is suggested from without, it commends itself as the one true interpretation, from its appositeness,—because no other view of doctrine, which can be ascribed to the inspired writers, so happily solves the obscurities and seeming inconsistencies of their teaching. And now to apply what I have said to the passage in the Apocalypse.

If there is an Apostle on whom, *à priori,* our eyes would be fixed, as likely to teach us about the Blessed Virgin, it is St. John, to whom she was committed by our Lord on the Cross;—with whom, as tradition goes, she lived at Ephesus till she was taken away. This anticipation is confirmed *à posteriori;* for, as I have said above, one of the earliest and fullest of our informants concerning her dignity, as being the **Second Eve**, is Irenæus, who came to Lyons from Asia Minor, and had been taught by the immediate disciples of St. John. The Apostle's vision is as follows: —

"**A great sign appeared in heaven: A woman clothed with the Sun, and the Moon under her feet; and on her head a crown of twelve stars. And being with child, she cried travailing in birth, and was in pain to be delivered. And there was seen another sign in heaven; and behold a great red dragon . . . And the dragon stood before the woman who was ready to be delivered, that, when she should be delivered, he might devour her son. And she brought forth a man child, who was to rule all nations with an iron rod; and her**

17

son was taken up to God and to His throne. And the woman fled into the wilderness." Now I do not deny of course, that, under the image of the Woman, the Church is signified; but what I would maintain is this, that the Holy Apostle would not have spoken of the Church under this particular image, *unless* there had existed a Blessed Virgin Mary, who was exalted on high, and the object of veneration to all the faithful.

No one doubts that the **"man-child"** spoken of is an allusion to our Lord: why then is not **"the Woman"** an allusion to His Mother? This surely is the obvious sense of the words; of course it has a further sense also, which is the scope of the image; doubtless the Child represents the children of the Church, and doubtless the Woman represents the Church; this, I grant, is the real or direct sense, but what is the sense of the symbol? *who* are the Woman and the Child? I answer, They are not personifications but Persons. This is true of the Child, therefore it is true of the Woman.

But again: not only Mother and Child, but a serpent is introduced into the vision. Such a meeting of man, woman, and serpent has not been found in Scripture, since the beginning of Scripture, and now it is found in its end. Moreover, in the passage in the Apocalypse, as if to supply, before Scripture came to an end, what was wanting in its beginning, we are told, and for the first time, that the serpent in Paradise was the evil spirit. If the dragon of St. John is the same as the serpent of Moses, and the man-child is **"the seed of the woman"**, why is not the woman herself she, whose seed the man-child is? And, if the first woman is not an allegory, why is the second? if the first woman is Eve, why is not the second Mary?

But this is not all. The image of the woman, according to Scripture usage, is too bold and prominent for a mere personification. Scripture is not fond of allegories. We have indeed frequent figures there, as when the sacred writers speak of the arm or sword of the Lord; and so too when they speak of Jerusalem or Samaria in the feminine; or of the mountains leaping for joy; or of the Church as a bride or as a vine; but they are not much given to dressing up abstract ideas or generalizations in personal attributes. This is the classical rather than the Scriptural style. Xenophon places Hercules between Virtue and Vice, represented as women; Æschylus introduces into his drama Force and Violence; Virgil gives personality to public rumour or Fame, and Plautus to Poverty. So on monuments done in the classical style, we see virtues, vices, rivers, renown, death and the like, turned into human figures of men and women. I do not say there are no instances at all of this method in Scripture, but I say that such poetical compositions are strikingly unlike its usual method. Thus we at once feel its difference from Scripture, when we betake ourselves to the Pastor of Hermes, and find the Church a woman; to St. Methodius, and find Virtue a woman; and to St. Gregory's poem, and find Virginity again a woman. Scripture deals with types rather than personifications. Israel stands for the chosen people, David for Christ, Jerusalem for heaven. . . .

Coming back then to the Apocalyptic vision, I ask, If the Woman must be some real person, who can it be whom the Apostle saw, and intends, and delineates, but that same Great Mother to whom the chapters in the Proverbs are accommodated? And let it be observed, moreover, that in this passage, from the allusion in it to the history of the fall, she may be said still to be represented under the character of the **Second Eve**. I make a further remark: it is sometimes asked, Why do not the sacred writers mention our Lady's greatness? I answer, She was, or may have been, alive, when the Apostles and Evangelists wrote;—there was just one book of Scripture certainly written after her death, and that book does (if I may so speak) canonize her.

But if all this be so, if it is really the Blessed Virgin whom Scripture represents as clothed with the sun, crowned with the stars of heaven, and with the moon as her footstool, what height of glory may we not attribute to her? and what are we to say of those who, through ignorance, run counter to the voice of Scripture, to the testimony of the Fathers, to the traditions of East and West, and speak and act contemptuously towards her whom her Lord delighteth to honour? (I p. 59-66).

.   .   .

THEOTOCOS

It is then an integral portion of the Faith fixed by Ecumenical Council . . . that the Blessed Virgin is **Theotocos, Deipara,** or **Mother**

of God; and this word, when thus used, carries with it no admixture of rhetoric, no taint of extravagant affection,—it has nothing else but a well-weighed, grave, dogmatic sense, which corresponds and is adequate to its sound. It intends to express that God is her Son, as truly as any one of us is the son of his own mother. If this be so, what can be said of any creature whatever, which may not be said of her? what can be said too much, so that it does not compromise the attributes of the Creator? He indeed might have created a being more perfect, more admirable, than she is; He might have endued that being, so created, with a richer grant of grace, of power, of blessedness: but in one respect she surpasses all even possible creations, viz., that she is **Mother of her Creator**. . . . It is the issue of her sanctity; it is the source of her greatness. What dignity can be too great to attribute to her who is as closely bound up, as intimately one, with the Eternal Word, as a mother is with a son? What outfit of sanctity, what fulness and redundance of grace, what exuberance of merits must have been hers, on the supposition, which the Fathers justify, that her Maker regarded them at all, and took them into account, when he condescended not to abhor the Virgin's womb? Is it surprising then that on the one hand she should be immaculate in her Conception? or on the other that she should be honoured with an Assumption, and exalted as a queen with a crown of twelve stars, with the rulers of day and night to do her service? Men sometimes wonder that we call her Mother of life, of mercy, of salvation; what are all these titles compared to that one name, **Mother of God?** . . . (I p. 66-67).

.   .   .

The title of *Theotocos* begins with ecclesiastical writers of a date hardly later than that at which we read of her as the Second Eve. It first occurs in the works of Origen (185-254); but he, witnessing for Egypt and Palestine, witnesses also that it was in use before his time; for, as Socrates informs us, he "interpreted how it was to be used, and discussed the question at length" *(Hist.* vii. 32). Within two centuries (431) in the General Council held against Nestorius, it was made part of the formal dogmatic teaching of the Church. At that time, Theodoret, who from his party connexions might have been supposed disinclined to its solemn recognition, owned that "the ancient and more than ancient heralds of the orthodox faith taught the use of the term according to the Apostolic tradition." At the same date John of Antioch, who for a while sheltered Nestorius, whose heresy lay in the rejection of the term, said, "This title no ecclesiastical teacher has put aside. Those who have used it are many and eminent; and those who have not used it, have not attacked those who did." Alexander, again, one of the fiercest partisans of Nestorius, witnesses to the use of the word, though he considers it dangerous; "That in festive solemnities", he says, "or in preaching or teaching, *theotocos* should be unguardedly said by the orthodox without explanation is no blame, because such statements were not dogmatic, nor said with evil meaning." If we look for those, in the interval, between Origen and the Council, to whom Alexander refers, we find it used again and again by the Fathers in such of their works as are extant; by Archelaus of Mesopotamia, Eusebius of Palestine, Alexander of Egypt, in the third century; in the fourth by Athanasius many times with emphasis, by Cyril of Palestine, Gregory Nyssen of Cappadocia, Gregory Nazianzen of Cappadocia, Antiochus of Syria, and Ammonius of Thrace:—not to speak of the Emperor Julian, who, having no local or ecclesiastical domicile, speaks for the whole of Christendom. Another and earlier Emperor, Constantine, in his speech before the assembled Bishops at Nicæa, uses the still more explicit title of **"the Virgin Mother of God";** which is also used by Ambrose of Milan, and by Vincent and Cassian in the south of France, and then by St. Leo. . . .

"Our God was carried in the womb of Mary", says Ignatius, who was martyred A.D. 106. **"The Word of God",** says Hippolytus, **"was carried in that Virgin frame." "The Maker of all",** says Amphilochius, **"is born of a Virgin." "She did compass without circumscribing the Sun of justice,—the Everlasting is born",** says Chrysostom. **"God dwelt in the womb",** says Proclus. **"When thou hearest that God speaks from the bush",** asks Theodotus, **"in the bush seest thou not the Virgin?"** Cassian says, **"Mary bore her Author." "The One God only-begotten",** says Hilary, **"is introduced into the womb of a Virgin." "The Everlasting",** says Ambrose, **"came into the Virgin." "The closed gate",** says Jerome, **"by which alone the Lord God of Israel enters, is the Virgin Mary." "That man from heaven",** says Capriolus, **"is God conceived in the womb." "He is made in thee",** says Augustine, **"who made thee."**

21

This being the faith of the Fathers about the Blessed Virgin, we need not wonder that it should in no long time be transmuted into devotion. No wonder if their language should become unmeasured, when so great a term as **"Mother of God"** had been formally set down as the safe limit of it. No wonder if it became stronger and stronger as time went on, since only in a long period could the fulness of its import be exhausted. . . . **"She was alone, and wrought the world's salvation and conceived the redemption of all"**, says Ambrose; **"she had so great grace, as not only to preserve virginity herself, but to confer it upon those whom she visited." "The rod out of the stem of Jesse"**, says Jerome, **"and the Eastern gate through which the High Priest alone goes in and out, yet is ever shut."** (I p. 68-71).

. . .

Mary is called the *Gate* of Heaven, because it was through her that our Lord passed from heaven to earth. The Prophet Ezechiel, prophesying of Mary, says, **"The gate shall be closed, it shall not be opened, and no man shall pass through it, since the Lord God of Israel has entered through it—and it shall be closed for the Prince, the Prince Himself shall sit in it."**

Now this is fulfilled, not only in our Lord's having taken flesh from her, and being her Son, but moreover, in that she had a place in the economy of Redemption; it is fulfilled in her spirit and will, as well as in her body. . . . (II p. 51-52).

. . .

It was no light lot to be so intimately near to the Redeemer of men, as she experienced afterwards when she suffered with Him. Therefore, weighing well the Angel's words before giving her answer to them— first she asked whether so great an office would be a forfeiture of that Virginity which she had vowed. When the Angel told her no, then, with the full consent of a full heart, full of God's love to her and her own lowliness, she said, **"Behold the handmaid of the Lord,**

be it done unto me according to Thy word." It was by this consent that she became the *Gate of Heaven*. (II p. 53-54).

.　　.　　.

She is invoked by us as the *Mother of Christ*. What is the force of thus addressing her? It is to bring before us that she it is who from the first was prophesied of, and associated with the hopes and prayers of all holy men, of all true worshippers of God, of all who **"looked for the redemption of Israel"** in every age before that redemption came.

Our Lord was called the Christ, or the Messias, by the Jewish prophets and the Jewish people. The two words Christ and Messias mean the same. They mean in English the "Anointed". In the old time there were three great ministries or offices by means of which God spoke to His chosen people, the Israelites, or, as they were afterwards called, the Jews, viz., that of Priest, that of King, and that of Prophet. Those who were chosen by God for one or other of these offices were solemnly anointed with oil—oil signifying the grace of God, which was given to them for the due performance of their high duties. But our Lord was all three, a Priest, a Prophet, and a King— a Priest, because He offered Himself as a sacrifice for our sins; a Prophet, because He revealed to us the Holy Law of God; and a King, because He rules over us. Thus He is the one true Christ.

It was in expectation of this great Messias that the chosen people, the Jews, or Israelites, or Hebrews (for these are different names for the same people), looked out from age to age. He was to come to set all things right. And next to this great question which occupied their minds, namely, *When* was He to come, was the question, *Who* was to be His Mother? It had been told them from the first, not that He should come from heaven, but that He should be born of a woman. . . . Who, then, was to be that Woman thus significantly pointed out to the fallen race of Adam? At the end of many centuries, it was further revealed to the Jews that the great Messias, or Christ, the seed of the Woman, should be born of their race, and of one particular tribe of the twelve tribes into which that race was divided. From that time every woman of that tribe hoped to have the great privilege

23

of herself being the Mother of the Messias, or Christ; for it stood to reason, since He was so great, the Mother must be great, and good, and blessed too. Hence it was, among other reasons, that they thought so highly of the marriage state, because, not knowing the mystery of the miraculous conception of the Christ when He was actually to come, they thought that the marriage rite was the ordinance necessary for His coming.

Hence it was, if Mary had been as other women, she would have longed for marriage, as opening on her the prospect of bearing the great King. But she was too humble and too pure for such thoughts. She had been inspired to choose that better way of serving God which had not been made known to the Jews—the state of Virginity. She preferred to be His Spouse to being His Mother. Accordingly, when the Angel Gabriel announced to her her high destiny, she shrank from it till she was assured that it would not oblige her to revoke her purpose of a virgin life devoted to her God.

Thus was it that she became the Mother of Christ, not in that way which pious women for so many ages had expected Him, but, declining the grace of such maternity, she gained it by means of a higher grace. And this is the full meaning of St. Elizabeth's words, when the Blessed Virgin came to visit her, which we use in the Hail Mary: **"Blessed art thou among women, and blessed is the fruit of thy womb."** (II p. 59-63).

. . .

Mother of the Creator. This is a title which, of all others, we should have thought it impossible for any creature to possess. At first sight we might be tempted to say that it throws into confusion our primary ideas of the Creator and the creature, the Eternal and the temporal, the Self-subsisting and the dependent; and yet on further consideration we shall see that we cannot refuse the title to Mary without denying the Divine Incarnation—that is, the great and fundamental truth of revelation, that God became man.

And this was seen from the first age of the Church. Christians were accustomed from the first to call the Blessed Virgin **"The**

Mother of God", because they saw that it was impossible to deny her that title without denying St. John's words, **"The Word"** (that is, God the Son) **"was made flesh."**

And in no long time it was found necessary to proclaim this truth by the voice of an Ecumenical Council of the Church. For, in consequence of the dislike which men have of a mystery, the error sprang up that our Lord was not really God, but a man, differing from us in this merely—that God dwelt in Him, as God dwells in all good men, only in a higher measure; as the Holy Spirit dwelt in Angels and Prophets, as in a sort of Temple; or again, as our Lord now dwells in the Tabernacle in church. And then the bishops and faithful people found there was no other way of hindering this false, bad view being taught but by declaring distinctly, and making it a point of faith, that Mary was the Mother, not of man only, but of God. And since that time the title of Mary, as *Mother of God,* has become what is called a dogma, or article of faith, in the Church. (II p. 55-57).

.   .   .

. . . few Protestants have any real perception of the doctrine of God and man in one Person. They speak in a dreamy, shadowy way of Christ's divinity; but, when their meaning is sifted, you will find them very slow to commit themselves to any statement sufficient to express the Catholic dogma. . . . Then when they comment on the Gospels, they will speak of Christ, not simply and consistently as God, but as a being made up of God and man, partly one and partly the other, or between both, or as a man inhabited by a special divine presence. . . . and they are shocked, and think it a mark both of reverence and good sense to be shocked, when they hear the Man spoken of simply and plainly as God. They cannot bear to have it said, except as a figure or mode of speaking, that God had a human body, or that God suffered; they think that the **"Atonement"**, and **"Sanctification through the Spirit"**, as they speak, is the sum and substance of the Gospel, and they are shy of any dogmatic expression which goes beyond them. . . .

Now, if you would witness against these unchristian opinions, if you would bring out, distinctly and beyond mistake and evasion, the simple idea of the Catholic Church that God is man, could you do it better than by laying down in St. John's words that **"God *became"*** man? and could you express this again more emphatically and unambiguously than by declaring that He was *born* a man, or that He had a *Mother?* The world allows that God *is* man; the admission costs it little, for God is everywhere; and (as it may say) is everything; but it shrinks from confessing that God is the Son of Mary. It shrinks, for it is at once confronted with a severe fact, which violates and shatters its own unbelieving view of things; the revealed doctrine forthwith takes its true shape, and receives an historical reality; and the Almighty is introduced into His own world at a certain time and in a definite way. Dreams are broken and shadows depart; the truth of God is no longer a poetical expression, or a devotional exaggeration, or a mystical economy, or a mythical representation. **"Sacrifice and offering"**, the shadows of the Law, **"Thou wouldest not, but a body has Thou fitted to Me." "That which was from the beginning, which we have heard, which we have seen with our eyes, which we have diligently looked upon, and our hands have handled", "That which we have seen and have heard, declare we unto you";** such is the record of the Apostle, in opposition to those **"spirits"** which denied that **"Jesus Christ had appeared in the flesh",** and which **"dissolved"** Him by denying either His human nature or His divine. And the confession that Mary is ***Deipara,*** or the **Mother of God**, is that safeguard wherewith we seal up and secure the doctrine of the Apostle from all evasion, and that test whereby we detect all the pretences of those bad spirits of **"Antichrist which have gone out into the world."** It declares that He is God; it implies that He is man; it conveys to us that He is God still, though He has become man, and that He is true man though He is God. By witnessing to the *process* of the union, it secures the reality of the two *subjects* of it, of the divinity and of the manhood. If Mary is the Mother of God, Christ is understood to be Emmanuel, God with us. And hence it was, that, when time went on, and the bad spirits and false prophets grew stronger and bolder and found a way into the Catholic body itself, then the Church, guided by God, could find no more effectual and sure way of expelling them, than that of using the word ***Deipara*** against them; . . . (III p. 402-405).

.   .   .

The Prophet says, **"There shall come forth a rod out of the root of Jesse, and a flower shall rise out of his root."** Who is the flower but our Blessed Lord? Who is the rod, or beautiful stalk or stem or plant out of which the flower grows, but Mary, Mother of our Lord, Mary, Mother of God?

It was prophesied that God should come upon earth. When the time was now full, how was it announced? It was announced by the Angel coming to Mary. **"Hail, full of grace"**, said Gabriel, **"the Lord is with thee; blessed art thou among women."** (II p. 4-5).

.   .   .

And so of the great Mother of God, as far as a creature can be like the Creator; her ineffable purity and utter freedom from any shadow of sin, her Immaculate Conception, her ever-virginity—these her prerogatives (in spite of her extreme youth at the time when Gabriel came to her) are such as to lead us to exclaim in the prophetic words of Scripture, both with awe and with exultation, **"Thou art the glory of Jerusalem and the joy of Israel; thou art the honour of our people; therefore hath the hand of the Lord strengthened thee, and therefore art thou blessed for ever."** (II p. 35-36).

.   .   .

THE ASSUMPTION

By her Assumption is meant that not only her soul, but her body also, was taken up to heaven upon her death, so that there was no long period of her sleeping in the grave, as is the case with others, even great Saints, who wait for the last day for the resurrection of their bodies. (II p. 93).

.   .   .

One reason for believing in our Lady's Assumption is that her Divine Son loved her too much to let her body remain in the grave.

27

A second reason—that now before us—is this, that she was not only dear to our Lord as a mother is dear to a son, but also that she was so transcendently holy, so full, so overflowing with grace. Adam and Eve were created upright and sinless, and had a large measure of God's grace bestowed upon them, and, in consequence, their bodies would never have crumbled into dust, had they not sinned; upon which it was said to them, **"Dust thou art, and unto dust thou shalt return."** If Eve, the beautiful daughter of God, never would have become dust and ashes unless she had sinned, shall we not say that Mary, having never sinned, retained the gift which Eve by sinning lost? What had Mary done to forfeit the privilege given to our first parents in the beginning? Was her comeliness to be turned into corruption, and her fine gold to become dim, without reason assigned? Impossible. Therefore we believe that, though she died for a short hour, as did our Lord Himself, yet, like Him, and by His Almighty power, she was raised again from the grave.   (II p. 93-94).

.   .   .

Mary is the most beautiful flower that ever was seen in the spiritual world. It is by the power of God's grace that from this barren and desolate earth there have ever sprung up at all flowers of holiness and glory. And Mary is the Queen of them. She is the Queen of spiritual flowers; and therefore she is called the *Rose*, for the rose is fitly called of all flowers the most beautiful.

But moreover, she is the *Mystical*, or *hidden* rose; for mystical means hidden. How is she now "hidden" from us more than are other saints? What means this singular appellation, which we apply to her specially? The answer to this question introduces us to a third reason for believing in the reunion of her sacred body to her soul, and its assumption into heaven soon after her death, instead of its lingering in the grave until the General Resurrection at the last day.

It is this: —if her body was not taken into heaven, where is it? how comes it that it is hidden from us? why do we not hear of her tomb as being here or there? why are not pilgrimages made to it?

why are not relics producible of her, as of the saints in general? Is it not even a natural instinct which makes us reverent towards the places where our dead are buried? We bury our great men honourably. St. Peter speaks of the sepulchre of David as known in his day, though he had died many hundred years before. When our Lord's body was taken down from the Cross, He was placed in an honourable tomb. Such too had been the honour already paid to St. John Baptist, his tomb being spoken of by St. Mark as generally known. Christians from the earliest times went from other countries to Jerusalem to see the holy places. And, when the time of persecution was over, they paid still more attention to the bodies of the Saints, as of St. Stephen, St. Mark, St. Barnabas, St. Peter, St. Paul, and other Apostles and Martyrs. These were transported to great cities, and portions of them sent to this place or that. Thus, from the first to this day it has been a great feature and characteristic of the Church to be most tender and reverent towards the bodies of the Saints. Now, if there was anyone who more than all would be preciously taken care of, it would be our Lady. Why then do we hear nothing of the Blessed Virgin's body and its separate relics. Why is she thus the *hidden* Rose? Is it conceivable that they who had been so reverent and careful of the bodies of the Saints and Martyrs should neglect her—her who was the **Queen of Martyrs** and the **Queen of Saints**, who was the very Mother of our Lord? It is impossible. Why then is she thus the *hidden* Rose? Plainly because that sacred body is in heaven, not on earth.   (II p. 95-98).

. . .

As soon as we apprehend by faith the great fundamental truth that Mary is the Mother of God, other wonderful truths follow in its train; and one of these is that she was exempt from the ordinary lot of mortals, which is not only to die, but to become earth to earth, ashes to ashes, dust to dust. Die she must, and die she did, as her Divine Son died, for He was man; but various reasons have approved themselves to holy writers, why, although her body was for a while separated from her soul, and consigned to the tomb, yet it did not remain there, but was speedily united to her soul again, and raised by our Lord to a new and eternal life of heavenly glory.

And the most obvious reason for so concluding is this—that *other* servants of God have been raised from the grave by the power of God, and it is not to be supposed that our Lord would have granted any such privilege to anyone else without also granting it to His own Mother.

We are told by St. Matthew, that after our Lord's death upon the Cross **"the graves were opened, and many bodies of the saints that had slept"**—that is, slept the sleep of death—**"arose, and coming out of the tombs after His Resurrection, came into the Holy City, and appeared to many."** St. Matthew says, *"many* **bodies of the Saints"** —that is, the holy Prophets, Priests, and Kings of former times— rose again in anticipation of the last day.

Can we suppose that Abraham, or David, or Isaias, or Ezechias, should have been thus favoured, and not God's own Mother? Had she not a claim on the love of her Son to have what any others had? Was she not nearer to Him than the greatest of the Saints before her? And is it conceivable that the law of the grave should admit of relaxation in their case, and not in hers? Therefore we confidently say that our Lord, having preserved her from sin and the consequences of sin by His Passion, lost no time in pouring out the full merits of that Passion upon her body as well as her soul.   (II p. 89-91).

▫ • •

Another consideration which has led devout minds to believe in the Assumption of our Lady into heaven after her death, without waiting for the general resurrection at the last day, is furnished by the doctrine of her Immaculate Conception.   (II p. 92).

• • •

It was surely fitting, it was becoming, that she should be taken up into heaven and not lie in the grave till Christ's second coming, who had passed a life of sanctity and of miracle such as hers. All the works of God are in a beautiful harmony; they are carried on to the end as they begin. This is the difficulty which men of the world find

30

in believing miracles at all; they think these break the order and consistency of God's visible world, not knowing that they do but subserve to a higher order of things, and introduce a supernatural perfection. But at least, my brethren, when one miracle is wrought, it may be expected to draw others after it for the completion of what is begun. Miracles must be wrought for some great end; and if the course of things fell back again into a natural order before its termination, how could we but feel a disappointment? and if we were told that this certainly was to be, how could we but judge the information improbable and difficult to believe? Now this applies to the history of our Lady. I say, it would be a greater miracle, if, her life being what it was, her death was like that of other men, than if it were such as to correspond to her life. Who can conceive, my brethren, that God should so repay the debt which He condescended to owe to His Mother, for the elements of His human Body, as to allow the flesh and blood from which It was taken to moulder in the grave? Do the sons of men thus deal with their mothers? do they not nourish and sustain them in their feebleness, and keep them in life while they are able? Or who can conceive that that virginal frame, which never sinned, was to undergo the death of a sinner? Why should she share the curse of Adam, who had no share in his fall? **"Dust thou art, and into dust thou shalt return"**, was the sentence upon sin; she then who was not a sinner, fitly never saw corruption. She died then, my brethren, because even our Lord and Saviour died; she died, as she suffered, because she was in this world, because she was in a state of things in which suffering and death are the rule. She lived under their external sway; and as she obeyed Cæsar by coming for enrolment to Bethlehem, so did she, when God willed it, yield to the tyranny of death, and was dissolved into soul and body, as well as others. But though she died as well as others, she died not as others die; for, through the merits of her Son, by whom she was what she was, by the grace of Christ which in her had anticipated sin, which had filled her with light, which had purified her flesh from all defilement, she had been saved from disease and malady, and all that weakens and decays the bodily frame. Original sin had not been found in her, by the wear of her senses, and the waste of her frame, and the decrepitude of years, propagating death. She died, but her death was a mere fact, not an effect; and when it was over, it ceased to be. She died that she might live; she died as a matter of form or (as I may call it) a ceremony, in order to fulfil, what is called, the debt of nature—not primarily for herself or because of sin, but to submit herself to her condition, to glorify God, to do what her Son did; not however as her Son and Saviour, with any suffering for any special end; not with a martyr's death, for her martyrdom had been in living; not as an atonement, for man could not make it, and One had made it and made it for all; but in order to finish her course, and to receive her crown.

And therefore she died in private. It became Him, who died for the world, to die in the world's sight; it became the Great Sacrifice to be lifted up on high, as a light that could not be hid. But she, the lily of Eden, who had always dwelt out of the sight of man, fittingly did she die in the garden's shade, and amid the sweet flowers in which she had lived. Her departure made no noise in the world. The Church went about her common duties, preaching, converting, suffering; there were persecutions, there was fleeing from place to place, there were martyrs, there were triumphs; at length the rumour spread through Christendom that Mary was no longer upon earth. Pilgrims went to and fro; they sought for her relics, but they found them not; did she die at Ephesus? or did she die at Jerusalem? accounts varied; but her tomb could not be pointed out, or if it was found, it was open; and instead of her pure and fragrant body, there was a growth of lilies from the earth which she had touched. So, inquirers went home marvelling, and waiting for further light. And then the tradition came wafted westward on the aromatic breeze, how that when the time of her dissolution was at hand, and her soul was to pass in triumph before the judgment-seat of her Son, the Apostles were suddenly gathered together in one place, even in the Holy City, to bear part in the joyful ceremonial; how that they buried her with fitting rites; how that the third day, when they came to the tomb, they found it empty, and angelic choirs with their glad voices were heard singing day and night the glories of their risen Queen. But, however we feel towards the detail of this history (nor is there anything in it which will be unwelcome or difficult to piety) so much cannot be doubted, from the consent of the whole Catholic world and the revelations made to holy souls, that, as is befitting, she is, soul and body, with her Son and God in heaven, and that we are enabled to celebrate, not only her death, but her Assumption.   (III p. 435-439).

.   .   .

INTERCESSORY POWER

It was in prayer that the Church was founded. For ten days all the Apostles **"persevered with one mind in prayer and supplication, with the women, and Mary the Mother of Jesus, and with His brethren."** Then again at Pentecost **"they were all with one mind in one place"**; and the converts then made are said to have **"persevered in prayer"**. And when, after a while, St. Peter was seized and put in prison with a view to his being put to death, **"prayer was made without ceasing"** by the Church of God for him; and, when the angel released him, he took refuge in a house **"where many were gathered together in prayer"**. (I p. 74).

.   .   .

It would be preposterous to pray for those who are already in glory; but at least they can pray for us, and we can ask their prayers, and in the Apocalypse at least Angels are introduced both sending us their blessing and presenting our prayers before the Divine Presence. We read there of an angel who **"came and stood before the altar, having a golden censer"**; and **"there was given to him much incense, that he should offer of the prayers of all saints upon the golden altar which is before the Throne of God"**. On this occasion, surely the Angel (Michael, as the prayer in Mass considers him) performed the part of a great Intercessor or Mediator above for the children of the Church Militant below. Again, in the beginning of the same book, the sacred writer goes so far as to speak of **"grace and peace"** being sent to us, not only from the Almighty, but **"from the seven Spirits that are before His throne"**, thus associating the Eternal with the ministers of His mercies; and this carries us on to the remarkable passage of St. Justin, one of the earliest Fathers, who, in his Apology, says, **"To Him (God), and His Son who came from Him, and taught us these things, and the host of the other good Angels who follow and resemble Him, and the Prophetic Spirit, we pay veneration and homage."** Further, in the Epistle to the Hebrews, St. Paul introduces, not only Angels, but **"the spirits of the just"** into the sacred communion: **"Ye have come to Mount Sion, to the heavenly Jerusalem, to myriads of angels, to God the Judge of all, to the spirits of the just made perfect, and to Jesus the Mediator of the New Testament."**

33

What can be meant by having **"come to the spirits of the just"**, unless in some way or other they do us good, whether by blessing or by aiding us? that is, in a word, to speak correctly, by praying for us, for it is by prayer alone that the creature above can bless or aid the creature below.

Intercession thus being the first principle of the Church's life, next it is certain again, that the vital principle of that intercession, as an availing power, is, according to the will of God, sanctity. This seems to be suggested by a passage of St. Paul, in which the Supreme Intercessor is said to be **"the Spirit":**—**"the Spirit Himself maketh intercession for us; He maketh intercession for the saints according to God."** However, the truth thus implied, is expressly brought out in other parts of Scripture, in the form both of doctrine and of example. The words of the man born blind speak the common-sense of nature: —**"If any man be a worshipper of God, him He heareth."** And Apostles confirm them: —**"the prayer of a just man availeth much"**, and **"whatever we ask, we receive, because we keep His commandments."** Then, as for examples, we read of Abraham and Moses, as having the divine purpose of judgment revealed to them beforehand, in order that they might deprecate its execution. To the friends of Job it was said, **"My servant Job shall pray for you; his face I will accept."** Elias by his prayer shut and opened the heavens. Elsewhere we read of **"Jeremias, Moses, and Samuel";** and of **"Noe, Daniel, and Job",** as being great mediators between God and His people. One instance is given us, which testifies the continuance of so high an office beyond this life. Lazarus, in the parable, is seen in Abraham's bosom. It is usual to pass over this striking passage with the remark that it is a Jewish expression; whereas, Jewish belief or not, it is recognised and sanctioned by our Lord Himself. What do we teach about the Blessed Virgin more wonderful than this? Let us suppose, that, at the hour of death, the faithful are committed to her arms; but if Abraham, not yet ascended on high, had charge of Lazarus, what offence is it to affirm the like of her, who was not merely **"the friend"**, but the very **"Mother of God"?** (I p. 75-78).

.   .   .

I consider it impossible then, for those who believe the Church to be one vast body in heaven and on earth, in which every holy creature of God has his place, and of which prayer is the life, when once they recognise the sanctity and greatness of the Blessed Virgin, not to perceive immediately, that her office above is one of perpetual intercession for the faithful militant, and that our very relation to her must be that of clients to a patron, and that, in the eternal enmity which exists between the woman and the serpent, while the serpent's strength is that of being the Tempter, the weapon of the **Second Eve** and Mother of God is prayer.

As then these ideas of her sanctity and greatness gradually penetrated the mind of Christendom, so did that of her intercessory power follow close upon them and with them. (I p. 78-79).

. . .

The Help of Christians. Our glorious Queen, since her Assumption on high, has been the minister of numberless services to the elect people of God upon earth, and to His Holy Church. This title of **"Help of Christians"** relates to those services of which the Divine Office, while recording and referring to the occasion on which it was given her, recounts five, connecting them more or less with the Rosary.

The first was on the first institution of the Devotion of the Rosary by St. Dominic, when, with the aid of the Blessed Virgin, he succeeded in arresting and overthrowing the formidable heresy of the Albigenses in the South of France.

The second was the great victory gained by the Christian fleet over the powerful Turkish Sultan in answer to the intercession of Pope St. Pius V, and the prayers of the Associations of the Rosary all over the Christian world; in lasting memory of which wonderful mercy Pope Pius introduced her title **"Auxilium Christianorum"** into her Litany; and Pope Gregory XIII; who followed him, dedicated the first Sunday in October, the day of the victory, to Our Lady of the Rosary.

The third was, in the words of the Divine Office, **"the glorious victory won at Vienna, under the guardianship of the Blessed Virgin,** over the most savage Sultan of the Turks, who was trampling on the necks of the Christians; in perpetual memory of which benefit Pope Innocent XI dedicated the Sunday in the Octave of her Nativity as the feast of her *august Name.*"

The fourth instance of her aid was the victory over the innumerable force of the same Turks in Hungary on the Feast of St. Mary ad Nives, in answer to the solemn supplication of the Confraternities of the Rosary; on occasion of which Popes Clement XI and Benedict XIII gave fresh honour and privilege to the Devotion of the Rosary.

And the fifth was her restoration of the Pope's temporal power, at the beginning of this century, after Napoleon the First, Emperor of the French, had taken it from the Holy See; on which occasion Pope Pius VII set apart May 24, the day of this mercy, as the Feast of the *Help of Christians,* for a perpetual thanksgiving. (II p. 105-107).

. . .

DEVOTION

And so in His mercy He has given us a revelation of Himself by coming amongst us, to be one of ourselves, with all the relations and qualities of humanity, to gain us over. He came down from Heaven and dwelt amongst us, and died for us. All these things are in the Creed, which contains the chief things that He has revealed to us about Himself. Now the great power of the Rosary lies in this, that it makes the Creed into a prayer; of course, the Creed is in some sense a prayer and a great act of homage to God; but the Rosary gives us the great truths of His life and death to meditate upon, and brings them nearer to our hearts. And so we contemplate all the great mysteries of His life and His birth in the manger; and so too the mysteries of His suffering and His glorified life. But even Christians, with all their knowledge of God, have usually more awe than love of him, and the special virtue of the Rosary lies in the special way in which it looks at these mysteries; for with all our thoughts of Him are mingled thoughts of His Mother, and in the relations between Mother and Son we have set before us the Holy Family, the home in which God lived. Now the family is, even humanly considered, a sacred thing; how much more the family bound together by supernatural ties, and, above all, that in which God dwelt with His Blessed Mother. This is what I should most wish you to remember in future years. (IV p. 44-45).

.   .   .

I recollect some lines, the happiest, I think, which that author wrote, which bring out strikingly the reciprocity . . . of the respective devotions to Mother and Son: —

"But scornful men have coldly said
     Thy love was leading me from God;
And yet in this I did but tread
     The very path my Saviour trod.

"They know but little of thy worth
     Who speak these heartless words to me;
For what did Jesus love on earth
     One half so tenderly as thee?

"Get me the grace to love thee more;
     Jesus will give, if thou wilt plead;
And, Mother, when life's cares are o'er,
     Oh, I shall love thee then indeed.

"Jesus, when His three hours were run,
     Bequeathed thee from the Cross to me;
And oh! how can I love thy Son,
     Sweet Mother, if I love not thee?"

                                        (I p. 101-102).

.   .   .

As you revere the Fathers, so you revere the Greek Church; and here again we have a witness on our behalf, of which you must be aware as fully as we are, and of which you must really mean to give us the benefit. In proportion as this remarkable fact is understood, it will take off the edge of the surprise of Anglicans at the sight of our devotions to our Lady. It must weigh with them, when they discover that we can enlist on our side in this controversy those seventy millions (I think they so consider them) of Orientals, who are separated from our communion. Is it not a very pregnant fact that the Eastern Churches, so independent of us, so long separated from the West, so jealous for Antiquity, should even surpass us in their exaltation of the Blessed Virgin?   (I p. 95).

* * *

I went to Loreto with a simple faith, believing what I still more believed when I saw it. . . . He who floated the Ark on the surges of a world-wide sea, and enclosed in it all living things, who has hidden the terrestrial paradise, who said that faith might move mountains, who sustained thousands for forty years in a sterile wilderness, who transported Elias and keeps him hidden till the end, could do this wonder also.   (V p. 156).

* * *

I say then, when once we have mastered the idea, that Mary bore, suckled, and handled the Eternal in the form of a child, what limit is conceivable to the rush and flood of thoughts which such a doctrine involves? What awe and surprise must attend upon the knowledge, that a creature has been brought so close to the Divine Essence? It was the creation of a new idea and of a new sympathy, a new faith and worship, when the holy Apostles announced that God had become incarnate; and a supreme love and devotion to Him became possible, which seemed hopeless before that revelation. But, besides this, a second range of thoughts was opened on mankind, unknown before, and unlike any other, as soon as it was understood that that Incarnate God had a mother.   (I p. 88).

* * *

May that bright and gentle Lady, the Blessed Virgin Mary, overcome you with her sweetness, and revenge herself on her foes by interceding effectually for their conversion!   (I p. 123-124).

If you have enjoyed this book, consider making your next selection from among the following ...

Prices subject to change.

Our Saviour and His Love for Us. *Garrigou-Lagrange, O.P.* 21.00
Providence. *Garrigou-Lagrange, O.P.* 18.50
Predestination. *Garrigou-Lagrange, O.P.* 18.50
The Soul of the Apostolate. *Dom Chautard* 12.50
Hail Holy Queen (from *Glories of Mary*). *St. Alphonsus* 9.00
Novena of Holy Communions. *Lovasik* 2.50
Brief Catechism for Adults. *Cogan* 12.50
The Cath. Religion—Illus./Expl. for Child, Adult, Convert. *Burbach* 12.50
Eucharistic Miracles. *Joan Carroll Cruz* 16.50
The Incorruptibles. *Joan Carroll Cruz* 16.50
Pope St. Pius X. *F. A. Forbes* 11.00
St. Alphonsus Liguori. *Frs. Miller and Aubin* 18.00
Self-Abandonment to Divine Providence. *Fr. de Caussade, S.J.* 22.50
The Song of Songs—A Mystical Exposition. *Fr. Arintero, O.P.* 21.50
Prophecy for Today. *Edward Connor* 7.50
Saint Michael and the Angels. *Approved Sources* 9.00
Dolorous Passion of Our Lord. *Anne C. Emmerich* 18.00
Modern Saints—Their Lives & Faces, Book I. *Ann Ball* 21.00
Modern Saints—Their Lives & Faces, Book II. *Ann Ball* 23.00
Our Lady of Fatima's Peace Plan from Heaven. *Booklet* 1.00
Divine Favors Granted to St. Joseph. *Père Binet* 7.50
St. Joseph Cafasso—Priest of the Gallows. *St. John Bosco* 6.00
Catechism of the Council of Trent. *McHugh/Callan* 27.50
The Foot of the Cross. *Fr. Faber.* 18.00
The Rosary in Action. *John Johnson* 12.00
Padre Pio—The Stigmatist. *Fr. Charles Carty* 16.50
Why Squander Illness? *Frs. Rumble & Carty* 4.00
The Sacred Heart and the Priesthood. *de la Touche* 10.00
Fatima—The Great Sign. *Francis Johnston* 12.00
Heliotropium—Conformity of Human Will to Divine. *Drexelius* 15.00
Charity for the Suffering Souls. *Fr. John Nageleisen* 18.00
Devotion to the Sacred Heart of Jesus. *Verheylezoon* 16.50
Who Is Padre Pio? *Radio Replies Press* 3.00
Child's Bible History. *Knecht* 7.00
The Stigmata and Modern Science. *Fr. Charles Carty* 2.50
The Life of Christ. 4 Vols. P.B. *Anne C. Emmerich* 75.00
St. Anthony—The Wonder Worker of Padua. *Stoddard* 7.00
The Precious Blood. *Fr. Faber* 16.50
The Holy Shroud & Four Visions. *Fr. O'Connell* 3.50
Clean Love in Courtship. *Fr. Lawrence Lovasik* 4.50
St. Martin de Porres. *Giuliana Cavallini* 15.00
The Secret of the Rosary. *St. Louis De Montfort* 5.00
The History of Antichrist. *Rev. P. Huchede* 4.00
St. Catherine of Siena. *Alice Curtayne* 16.50
Where We Got the Bible. *Fr. Henry Graham* 8.00
Hidden Treasure—Holy Mass. *St. Leonard* 7.50
Imitation of the Sacred Heart of Jesus. *Fr. Arnoudt* 18.50
The Life & Glories of St. Joseph. *Edward Thompson* 16.50
Père Lamy. *Biver.* 15.00
Humility of Heart. *Fr. Cajetan da Bergamo* 9.00
The Curé D'Ars. *Abbé Francis Trochu* 24.00

At your Bookdealer or direct from the Publisher.

Toll-Free 1-800-437-5876   *Fax 815-226-7770*
Tel. 815-226-7777   *www.tanbooks.com*

Prices subject to change.